Introduction

Life is hard, and every day we face challenges that need to be overcome, and we have a decision to make. Do we allow these challenges to take away our joy?

Growing up with a sister with intellectual and physical disabilities has taught me that challenges are always waiting, even at a young age, but even in the midst of those challenges we still have the ability to laugh. And the Thompsons laugh a lot!

Hali's and my lives are intertwined; in fact, my real name is Hali's Brother. We have been through everything together, and now it's time to share those stories with you. Over the years we have experienced many, what we call, Hali Stories. These are stories that can only be explained by having a Hali, and while some of them carry a deeper meaning on life, they are all funny in their own way.

Early on our family realized the importance of laughter, and the power it can have in the darkest of situations. We live with the belief that life is serious enough; we don't have to add to it.

Our journey as siblings has been adventurous to say the least, and we are excited to share this adventure with you! This is not an expert's opinion on how you should live your life; it's just a collection of stories that I have experienced because I have Hali as my sister. You could consider me a jack-of-all-trades, with little expertise in most areas. One thing I know for sure, I am an expert at being Hali's Brother, and it's only taken me 28 years!

I encourage you to laugh while you read this book, and through the laughter, just know that we thank you for sharing in this journey with us!

Justin Thompson

CONTENTS

ACKNOWLEDGMENTS

I would like to personally thank Teresa Kenedy for editing, I know it wasn't easy, and I greatly appreciate her work!
I would also like to thank the Perkins Family for helping me provide something that is relevant! I could not have made this happen if it were not for people like Teresa and the Perkins!!

I CALLED SHOTGUN!! is written in the memory, and honor of the entire village of people who have helped our family through the worst and best times of our life! Thank you, because without you, this book would not exist!

Chapter 1: I Called Shotgun

It all started when Hali got to the age that she realized sitting in the front seat was an honor. Up until this point, I would sit in the front, Hali would get in the back, and there wasn't anything made of it. However, almost overnight, she went from being ok with sitting in the back to fighting, to the bitter end, to sit in the front.

I don't know who taught her about shotgun, but I would like for you to announce yourself and apologize to my parents. There was a long stretch of time when they would dread the moment we had to get in the car. I didn't mind the fight because, as you will find out, I liked picking fights with Hali to ruffle her feathers.

So, the first time Hali called shotgun it caught us all off guard, and being the great brother that I am, I sat in the front seat anyway. She spent the next five minutes quoting me the rules of shotgun and trying to pull me out of the front seat. Finally, I gave it up.

Because my parents made me.

From there the battle was on. Calling shotgun became the ultimate strategy game in the Thompson house, which at one point involved my parents telling Hali to come in my room and call it the night before we went to school. It got to the point that if Hali lost she would call it for the next several days. It became so ridiculous that we actually made our own house rules as to when you could actually call shotgun. Hali didn't care; she was not going to lose, and it really frustrated her when she would call it and Mom would sit in the front, mainly because she saw it as a battle against the guys, and she wasn't about to go against the other girl on her team.

The battle would go on for several years. It involved running to the garage and sitting in the seat before the other one could call it followed by the other one trying to pull open the door along with the arm of the one sitting in the seat.

Hali became really good at the game. She would sneak into the garage and call it out loud before I was even ready (the rule was that we had to be in the garage.) Yep, she got me several times.

The tension eased when I moved away for college. Her turf was finally secured and she never had to worry about it again...

Then the unthinkable happened.

I moved back in with my parents.

I know what you are thinking; you moved back in when you were 25?

That is correct.

It took some adjusting, but we finally worked it out...
when I moved into my own place a few years later.

I had forgotten this story until I came across an old journal.
I was reading through my different writings and came across one
about a future book idea entitled: I CALLED SHOTGUN!!: A Life
in the Backseat. How amazing is it that 6 years ago I was already
thinking about what I am currently doing, writing about life with
Hali.

I have to be honest, I didn't have to take the backseat as
often as it may seem, but there have been several times in my life
where it felt like I did. As I think about it today it seems petty, but
what's life if it isn't a little petty at times.

This is the perfect story to start with because it gives you a
glimpse of our life. Yes, there were things that made us different
from most siblings. Those would be the things like staying awake
during the night, at the age of 10, to listen for Hali having a
seizure, and spending a couple of months of my senior year going
to the hospital after school to be with her during her surgeries. Or,
receiving an air mattress for our wedding gift because when Mom
and Dad are out of town she stays with us. Or, becoming a legal
guardian, at the age of 25, to your sister who is only 18 months
younger than you...

Come to think of it, there are several things that set us apart from other siblings, and this book will highlight those things from my perspective. However, there are also several things that make us as typical as any brother and sister, and those stories are not only hilarious, they are epic.

In my life, I have often spent so much time focusing on what makes us different that sometimes I forget that I was created to be more than only Hali's Brother. Hali has taught us many things in her lifetime, and I was forced to learn early on that sometimes we just have to take the backseat for someone else.

Taking the backseat isn't only for siblings of people with special needs. It happens all of the time in our daily lives. There are times when I have had a long day, and my daughter wants to play outside, so we play outside. There are times when a student needs extra help on an assignment and the only time they can get the help is right after a night class. There are times when someone in need approaches you and you have to decide if you are going to put your life on hold to help them, or are you going to place yourself as the top priority?

We are faced with these decisions every day, I just happened to learn this lesson from having Hali as my sister, and I, too often, decide to place myself in the front seat.

This life isn't about us; it's about what we do for others, and it's hard to serve from the front seat.

Chapter 2: Strategic Planning

You know those things that people refer to as "life lessons?" Well, we have a few of them, and this one really began what we call "Hali Stories."

I was in the 5th grade, which means Hali was in the 3rd. Our great grandpa, Grandpa Day, had just passed away and we were attending the first funeral for a family member that I can remember. Leading up to the service, Hali had been hearing people say "We lost Grandpa," and she took it as we couldn't find him. So the day comes, we walk in as a family and Hali gets seated right behind Grandma Day. As the service gets started, you can see Hali looking up at the open casket and leaning back with a look of surprise. We can all see the wheels turning as she thinks about what she just saw.

She leans up and takes another peek, to be sure, and sits back in her seat.

She leans forward again and taps on Grandma Day's shoulder. Then, while everyone is quiet and having their moment, Hali tells Grandma Day, "Hey Grandma, I found your husband. He's in there!"

Hali provided a much-needed relief that day, and because of that, we now know that when you have a Hali, placement at a funeral is no light matter.

I use this story because it usually makes us laugh, and because it's the perfect story to illustrate the challenges that having a Hali can bring along the way. Our life is not what we would have imagined it being. Granted, we are only 18 months apart so I really have no idea what life without Hali would look like, but I'm pretty sure we wouldn't have to strategically plan a seating chart for funerals.

I can't remember where I heard this quote, but I love it because it fits so well with our families and I'm a creature of habit so I need to be reminded of it myself:

"The only constant in this life is change."

We are always adapting to new things being thrown at us. Our days usually start with a picture of how we think it will play out, and how often does it actually happen that exact way? If it's anything like my days, not often. We have an opportunity, on a daily basis, to learn from a new situation, and do we take that advantage? My parents had no know idea that Hali was going to react the way she did at her first funeral for a family member.

By no means does this make it an embarrassing moment; sure we all turned red, but we learned from it. More importantly, we learned to laugh about it, because it was only the beginning.

Truthfully, there have been many times when I have been embarrassed by my sister. It's part of it, but I have to ask myself during those moments if it's a Hali problem or a Justin problem. Although it pains me to say it, it's usually a Justin problem because I have this picture in my head of how something should look or go.

I have to be ok with Hali being who she is.

If I'm not, then Hali can't be ok with who she is.

When we were in school we went to a church camp every summer. It was another one of those terrifying moments for my family when Hali became a camper. We were headed toward uncharted territory and had no idea how it would go. Faithfully, my parents signed her up and just let it happen (with a ton of planning behind the scenes from my mom).

Every summer was the same. We ate the same things on the same days, had the same activities, etc. One of those activities was an overnight campout. The boys' cabins would pair up with a girls' cabin and we would hike out to a spot. We would play games and hang out around the campfire while our suppers cooked. During one of Hali's campouts she was sitting around the fire with some of the girls along with, some boys from their age group.

As Hali would typically do, she carried the conversation. Just FYI, Hali doesn't stop talking. EVER. She even talks in her sleep. On this night she said something that I guess was really out there and one of the boys responded by saying that it was stupid.

In perfect Hali fashion, she replied, "It's ok if I say stupid things sometimes."

I have no idea who this boy was, or what he's doing today, but I can assure you that he's never forgotten the time he was left speechless by a person he probably considered less than himself. And those girls? For the next 8 years those girls would build a bond with Hali that still continues.

If my parents are not ok with Hali being Hali, that story never happens. Those bonds are never built, and we missed out on a great opportunity.

We never know what will happen when we wake up each day, and we have a choice to make. We can both learn from it and continue our journey, or we can allow those moments to bind us until we become stuck.

Trust me, 30 years ago, we could have never imagined that it mattered where Hali sat during a funeral.

Chapter 3: Not That Big of a Deal

It all started when Hali and I were staying with our grandparents. Hali had a pretty severe seizure and my grandparents went straight into panic mode. And rightfully so. That situation was foreign to them. They weren't naïve to the fact that Hali had seizures, but they had never been in the same room when she had one. As soon as she started shaking they were dialing the phone to get a hold of my parents, who were on a plane. One voicemail after another was left. They finally gave the phone to me to, yep you guessed correctly, leave another voicemail.

My parents finally landed, thank goodness! Dad turned his phone back on and started listening.

First one, "Brad, this is your dad! Hali is having a seizure and we need to know what to do. I can't believe you would leave her with us!" Even though they loved having us, and took us every chance they got, seizures included.

Second one, "Brad, this is your mom! We don't know what to do and we are taking Hali to the emergency room!"

Final message, "Hey Dad, Hali had a seizure. She is fine and it's not a big deal. I tried to tell them she didn't need to go to the hospital because it would be over, but they didn't listen to me."

Well, it is and it isn't. Epilepsy is a big deal, especially when it can't be controlled. In this instance, however, I knew exactly what to do because I had been there before. I knew what to do in that moment. It wasn't that I was a genius or was unbelievably calm in a hectic situation, it was because, by that point, I had watched my parents handle the exact same situation multiple times.

I had even had to do it in the middle of the night, and early in the morning, while my parents were in a different room. At that moment it wasn't a big deal because my stress threshold had been built to withstand it.

Now this is a big deal.

At one point Hali was relatively healthy, with the exception of her severe epilepsy, up until high school. Since that time Hali's health has declined, and she lives in almost constant pain.

Watching her go through 5 brain surgeries, within the span of a year, was one of the hardest times in my life. She went in before Christmas for a surgery to fix a malformation in her brain.

I'd use the technical term, but I don't want to spell it and it would only add to the thought that I'm a terminology elitist. It wasn't an easy surgery, but it was supposed to be a one-time deal and we'd be home for Christmas.

Well, a few days in recovery eventually became almost 3 months with a slight break on Christmas Eve, though we returned Christmas day. At least Santa got to make a visit! She lost a lot of weight while I gained it because people were bringing us meals since Mom and Dad were constantly at the hospital, and I was spending my evenings after school at the hospital.

Our lives were turned upside down for a few months, and along the journey we built up an attitude about the common cold. Hali had a wonderful doctor and her nurses were great, but each day was touch and go. Thus, the medical terminology just began to infiltrate our lexicon.

Following that experience, it became tough for me to hear about people missing class or work because of a cough with a headache. Just take some Excedrin and get back to work!

To this day, I struggle with it. I know what sick is, so why should I stress about a cold? Now that I have a child of my own, I have realized that the things I experienced with Hali in 2005-2006 have shaped my view of struggle and sickness.

And, yes, I am a snob when it comes down to it. I just don't think it's that big of a deal most of the time, and trust me I've already worked through it.

However, also because of that experience, I overanalyze everything.

Do you know why? Because if Hali had a headache it wasn't just a headache, it was something deeper. Even before this we always had to be careful if she got sick because a fever would increase her seizure activity.

It's funny how when I look back, I can see what God was doing in my life because I wouldn't be a Strategic Analyst if I didn't overanalyze everything.

The cool thing is, if He did it for me, He will definitely do it for you! I know it may not offer any sense of relief in the moment; it never did for me either, but one day you will look back and see how everything played for a specific purpose.

Internal conflicts are something that I experience on a daily basis. Truthfully, I owe most of it to my sister. So if you're growing tired of hearing the response "Welllllll..." to your yes/no question, you may share your grievances with her.

And, know that it stresses me out just as much as it does you. Though, if you ever want to take something that seems like it's only a surface issue and hash it out beyond reasonable thought, I'm your person.

See, our experiences shape who we become. In some ways, this can be scary, but I believe, without a shadow of a doubt, that we have all been placed in a specific situation for a specific purpose. It doesn't have to be a Hali to make that true. My parents didn't have siblings with special needs, and yet, they were exactly where they needed to be for The Story to be told through them.

You are the only person with your perspective. Sure, there are millions of siblings of individuals with special needs, but there's not another Hali's Brother. I own that perspective, and I have been created to use that perspective to add to the greatest story of all. The story cannot be told without Hali, and Hali's story cannot be told without her brother.

What is your story? And is it the story of a life being lived to its fullest?

And don't ever miss work because of a cough... I'm kidding, BECAUSE IT COULD BE SOMETHING ELSE CAUSING THE COLD TO OCCUR WITH HIGHER SEVERITY AND FREQUENCY.

Justin Thompson

Chapter 4: Package Deal

"Till death do us, part" is a package deal, because Monica didn't just get me on that day. She also got Hali.

Why is that? Because on March 7, 2013 I walked out of my bedroom for the first time as a 25 year old. The first person I saw was my sister and decided that there was no better time to announce the greatest news I'd had in a while.

I said, "Hali do you know what today is?"

Knowing that it was my birthday, and the entire day was going to be about me, instead of her, she grunted, "Yessssss."

"And, do you know what that means?"

Immediately stopping what she was doing, she looked up and asked, "What?"

"That means that, as of today, I'm your boss!!!"

It was a big day for me because it really was the day I became her official guardian should anything happen to Mom and Dad. Hali always had a way of stealing my spotlight, and I knew that this was the one thing she couldn't take away from me. There was always a battle for who was in charge when Mom and Dad weren't around; my time had come and with law on my side I was really confident in my small victory.

But, without missing a beat, my sister looked at me, put her hand on her hip, cocked it to the side and responded, "Oh yeah JT, you may be my boss, but that just means that you have to get me everywhere I need to be!"

Victory…vacated.

It's a great story and always gets a laugh, but at the same time it is one of the truest statements she has ever made. In order to be Hali's brother I don't get to just be her boss, I also take on all of the responsibilities that are required to allow her to live her life to its fullest potential. Do you know how many places she needs to be? Oh my word!! It ain't an easy thing to get her everywhere she needs to be.

Hali and I are linked until the end of time.

This wasn't something that snuck up on me. I had been thinking about this almost my entire life. I knew, early on, that Hali would never be able to live on her own and would most likely live with me at some point in our lives.

My mom reminded me that when I was in elementary school I was already making plans for Hali. I told my parents that I was going to rent the dorm room next to me so that Hali could go to college with me. Looking back, even then, I realized that one day I was going to leave the house, and it wasn't likely that Hali would be able to do the same.

One of the things that having a sister like Hali does is force you to start thinking outside of yourself at a very early age. We all have those moments when we realize that there is more to this life than just ourselves, and for me, Hali was my awakening moment. Trust me, I'm not more gifted in this area than others; I only had to learn it earlier in my life because of my situation.

As I grew into the dating phase, I noticed that during the first date when I would get asked to tell them about myself I typically started with, I have a sister with special needs. Why? For one thing, it was how I defined my life for a good part of my growing up. Hali was so much a part of my life, and none of my friends had sisters like mine. I felt like being Hali's brother was who I was, and nothing more. But I also knew that if they couldn't handle it, then I didn't need to waste my time.

The truth is you can have Hali without Justin, but you can't have Justin without Hali. She is that part of my life that cannot be glossed over, or left out.

This realization wasn't easy for me; I struggled. There were times when I wanted a life that was just mine. I wanted to just be Justin. I didn't want the extra responsibility that comes with having a Hali. I looked for outlets where I didn't have to announce to everyone that Hali was my sister. The biggest struggle I am working through, however, is perfectionism.

My entire life I worried about messing up, because I lived in this pressure filled vacuum where if I did, it would add more stress to my parents who were already dealing with the extra stress of having a Hali. In fairness, it wasn't anything that anyone did to create this sense; it was mostly internal pressure I put on myself to achieve to a point where people didn't have to waste their worry on me.

Eventually it led me to searching for ways to relieve the pressure that weren't healthy. I was running away from the life I had been given, and it wasn't working out very well. I didn't shun my family during this time, but I was on a course to create my own story my own way. It's funny now because living in this way actually creates more worry than messing up. Looking back, it is crazy the amount of stress I put on my family by bottling things up until they exploded.

I would love to tell you that the pressure and responsibility went away, but they haven't. I still feel that way, but now I know why this is the life I have been given and I don't run away from it. I embrace this life, and when searching for that person to join my race I had to be certain they were on board as well.

Then came Monica. We started talking/dating right around the time I turned 25 so everything was fresh on my mind. I filled her in as best as I could; I mean there are things that can't be explained only experienced.

During our time together she has loved Hali like a sister and has never blinked at the reality of our package deal. If you are ever in need of laughter, invite H and JT over, and I can assure you that you will be entertained for that evening!

I constantly feel blessed that Monica is in my life, and there are several times that make it even more so. Recently, my parents had to make an emergency trip out of town and Hali needed somewhere to stay. I get the call from my mom and in that moment I felt a great sense of relief because I knew that when I called Monica to let her know, that she would embrace the situation.

If it had been anyone else, I might have been reluctant to make that call. There is no greater feeling in this world than knowing I have someone on this journey with me on a daily basis who allows me to be safe enough to make a call like that. Sure, there are many others who help, and have helped me along the way, but it's on a different level with Monica.

If Hali moves in with me, it's not just me. It's Monica and Ella as well. At any moment our unit could become plus one and that's our reality. Which is why I asked Monica to marry me in front of people! I trapped her!

The hard truth is that we are all part of a package deal. The question then becomes, with whom do we surround ourselves?

I heard a great thought on the radio, and since have heard it elsewhere. You are the average of the five people in your closest group of friends. This is great news if you surround yourself with great people, but what if you don't?

Do you surround yourself with people who are ok with Hali being a part of the group as well? Do you surround yourself with people who help you write your story along with Hali's? These are questions that are tough to answer, but in our lives, we have to ask them because Hali has to be able to belong alongside us.

Yes, as the sibling of someone with special needs, we are part of a package deal. But, the question we need to spend more time answering is, who are the people who are going to help you write your part of this story?

Chapter 5: Orientation Packet

I can remember my first day of training at Cal Farley's Boys Ranch like it was yesterday. I walk into this room with a few new employees and awkwardly pick a seat by the folks who will be my best friends for the next couple of weeks. Our trainer, Suzanne, walks in and starts passing out the one-inch binders of information about the organization. We start on page one going through policies and procedures, learning the Model of Leadership and Service. I thought to myself that this was a lot of information, but then I remembered that I had seen something similar in my life before…

My sister's emergency information.

Suddenly, I felt right at home.

You know you have a Hali when the emergency information for your sister isn't a sheet, but a packet filled with the list of doctors matched with their area of expertise, the list of medications with the times each one should be taken, and her insurance information.

I consider this the bible of Hali. It has been in every backpack and briefcase I have owned. I don't even travel without it because I know that the one moment I don't have it is the very moment I will need it. It's the moment when Mom and Dad can't be reached and it is my time to shine!

My Hali orientation was very similar to the experience I would have at Boys Ranch years later. Hali and I were in high school and our parents were going on a cruise.

They purposefully decided to take this cruise during the semester so that way they could just tell us we couldn't go because of school. That is how it happened, at least from my perspective.

In my head I have pictured them looking at their calendars for the perfect date that would allow them the easiest explanation for why we couldn't go with them. Oh, let's pick a week during school, then they'll be distracted by the fact that they know they can't miss school and it will be a very short conversation.

So, about 2 weeks before they left, Mom began going over everything in the packet. I felt like I was in an exam review. If this should happen, this is who you call, and this is what you tell them. When they ask for her medications, these are the medications she takes, at these times, and the dosage of each. If her head is hurting you can give her this much of this, and if it doesn't help, then call here.

Oh, she needs to be here at this time and there on these days. Don't worry, she won't let you forget, just make sure she is dressed appropriately and her hair is brushed.

I was 16.

I barely knew how to dress myself appropriately. I still thought jeans were okay for every occasion, and an ironed shirt (of any kind) was formal because it was pressed. This actually drove my dad crazy for years, because he ironed everything and couldn't stand the fact that I didn't care if it was or not. I have come a long way since those days, and now I do the ironing. See, parents, eventually we do come around!

This was the first time we had been left completely on our own, but it wasn't the first time my parents had been gone. They have been in ministry our entire lives, so travel was just part of our life; however, we usually stayed with grandparents when they were gone.

My mom had every reason to go through the smallest details with me, because it never failed that something would happen with Hali once one of our parents left town. And, with Hali, things weren't as simple as just a cold.

As I've talked about, there are a lot of moving parts when it comes to the care of Hali, and I had no choice but to be ready for anything. I mean my parents not only chose a vacation during school, they also chose a form of vacation that didn't allow easy contact.

At that moment, I had a choice. I could embrace the challenge, or I could run from it. In a naïve way, I felt that it was my responsibility to step up to the plate for my parents, and I also knew that nobody could do it better than me.

25

Plus, I thought it would also be cool to tell people that I was taking care of Hali while my parents were out of town. By the time I graduated from Mom's Hali orientation I felt ready; what did I really have to worry about? I had a booklet of names and numbers to help me through anything!

I still carry that information packet with me, and I add to it when things change.

Growing up with Hali forced me to look at life through a different lens. There are certain things that I just don't worry about because of my experiences with Hali.

You put me in a situation where I am familiar and I can be thrown anything without fear, but the unfamiliar brings about a whole new experience with which I don't do well. Even when it's a new challenge for Hali, I'm not as concerned because we have been facing new challenges with Hali for her entire life.

It's the fear of the unfamiliar which poses the greatest threat. It can cause us to abandon all of our beliefs about who is in control and forces us to rely just on our own abilities. I was forced to recognize this in my life a few years ago. I was at a point where for the first time in my life, my own ability just wasn't enough. I was in a marriage that wasn't working, and even after exhausting everything I could to make it work, I found myself living in an RV parked in the middle of a semi-truck sales lot.

At that moment, I had to come to the reality that I couldn't do it on my own.

Fear of not being in control led me down a path that I almost didn't come out of.

Fear is crippling because it drives us away from doing what we've been created to do. In my case, the challenges of everything that comes with Hali leaves me with a decision. I can either accept that this is the life given to me, or I can live in the denial that there is no purpose to be carried out.

To accept it means that I will face challenges on a regular basis, but the more challenges we face the more resilient we become. The end result is a life lived to the full and a story that will be told until the end of time.

To live in denial is allowing the fear to dictate our lack of living life to the fullest. There is a purpose for you, and this fear keeps you from realizing and living out that purpose.

I was created to be Hali's Brother, not only for Hali, but for all the other families who have a Hali as well.

And I can't run away from that.

Justin Thompson

Chapter 6: Constant Reminders

It all starts with one simple occurrence: our parents are out of town.

Which means Hali has staked her claim in La Casa de Younger Thompson. It really isn't a problem when she stays with us, and now that we have Ella it's even less of a problem because they both love playing with each other. Plus, as you now know, this is something that I have been doing since I was sixteen.

We have a great time! Of course, there is the ceremonial battle between us because she feels like since Mom and Dad aren't around that she should be able to do things that she would typically not do at home.

Unfortunately, for her, Mom will text both Monica and me to let us know what Hali can and can't eat. There may be a few times that she gets away with it, but that's only when we forget to ask Mom beforehand. Sometimes she makes me feel less like the responsible adult and more like the cool uncle that always delivers. But, at the end of the day, why not? It's a party when H arrives.

If you have ever given in to Hali's master plot, don't feel bad. I mean you probably should, to an extent, but don't lose sleep over it because you are part of a not-so elite club that dates back to middle school.

We usually took our lunch to school, but, for the few exceptions, Mom would put money in our account so we could eat lunch in the cafeteria. Knowing that my mom is the ultimate planner, you are probably guessing correctly that she would put an amount on our card that should get us all the way through the semester. She gets a call one day that Hali has run out of money on her account.

We went to a smaller school and my parents had no problems partnering with the staff to ensure we weren't goofing around. It paid off in this instance because there was no way Hali should have run out of money in this short amount of time, and it didn't help her case that we only ate in the cafeteria maybe once a week.

My mom can't believe that Hali has already run out of money so she asks the school counselor if she would keep an eye out for Hali during lunch. The counselor starts watching Hali. Hali had no idea of the plot against her, and I wish I could have seen this actually happen. As her brother, it is one of those moments that you hope for because you know she's going to be in trouble and it's the rare time when I didn't cause it.

Mom gets the call a few days later.

"Karen, you aren't going to believe this. Towards the end of lunch, one of the cafeteria workers wheels out a Little Debbie snack cart. Before she can even get the cart situated, Hali is in the front of the line. She gets a snack, sits down, and eats it. Then she goes back up to the cart to get another one!"

My sister had used her entire account to buy Little Debbie snacks!! She had fooled everyone! The real moral of the story? If you're doing something that you know your mom and dad wouldn't approve of, make sure that your money doesn't run out in a week.

And most of all, don't do it at a school where you know your mom and dad have had a conversation with every teacher/counselor that even has a chance of coming into contact with you at some point.

I share that with you to give you a glimpse of what we are dealing with here. Hali Thompson is a professional at convincing you its ok for her to eat something that she knows she shouldn't. So, in the event you ever find yourself in this trap, the following sentence is her kryptonite:

"Hali, let's ask your mom if it's ok that you have this."

Needless to say, we have a ton of fun when H comes to visit.

Even the great times can't keep me from having the re-occurring thought, however, that my parents have to put in a lot of work to be able to go out of town. Unlike the typical parents of adult children, they have to plan months ahead of time to make sure that Hali has a place to stay and is taken care of.

They don't have the luxury of deciding on a Friday afternoon to go out of town for the weekend just to have fun. If they decide on a Friday afternoon, it's the Friday afternoon two or more months ahead of time.

I don't know if it ever gets to a point when I stop seeing this as a reminder, but as for now, it is just a part of it.

It is crazy how single moments in life can have so many combating emotions wrapped up inside. Can a weekend with H just be fun without being a reminder? Can it just be thought of as a weekend that my sister is coming over? I don't know, I'm a work in progress.

Have you ever noticed how people have a need to relate things to something personal? It seems like we are always searching for ways that we can relate to something or someone else. Maybe you don't notice, or don't even care, but that random thought leads me to another reminder.

When people discover that a member of your family has special needs, they immediately begin thinking of other people they may know who are in the same boat. The most common is associating a celebrity connected with our community.

Fresh on my mind is the professional golfer, Jordan Spieth. He burst on the scene by winning quite a bit at a young age and with his celebrity status came the fact that he has a sister with special needs.

To this day, every time he wins a tournament and someone is talking to me about him they reference his sister, because they know that I have a sister with special needs.

It's in this moment that I am both excited, for him, and sorrowful because of the reminder. It is awesome when you get to see siblings be successful alongside their sibling with special needs, and we need more of those visible examples. I wonder if he ever has these same thoughts? I will most likely never get to have that conversation with him, but I am almost sure that he does.

Just like when Hali stays with us, we have a great time and truly it doesn't require much from me; it is just the fact that I have a sister who can't live on her own and needs to stay with someone.

Life's milestones are another harsh reminder, with school being one of the biggest contributors. Every August, Hali and I would start back to school after enjoying a great summer break, as most kids do. For me, it wasn't any big deal. It was just the next chapter in my story, and there wasn't much planning that needed to happen.

But for Hali, her school year had to be planned out beforehand through an Individualized Education Program [IEP]. This meant, that consistently, Mom and Dad would come up to the school and sit around a table with Hali's teachers, along with the school administration, and they would line out the goals for Hali in the upcoming year.

My dad remembers one specific meeting because as they walked out of it, he was pleased and somewhat excited about how the meeting had gone. Mom had a different reaction. Being the trained counselor that my dad is, he wanted to know what was going on. He asked her if something didn't go as well as he thought it had.

Mom responded, "No, everything went as well as expected. It has nothing to do with the meeting itself; it's the fact that every time we have one of these meetings it's a reminder that we have a Hali."

Hali has done some amazing things, and if you asked her, she wouldn't think that she has missed out on anything.

She went through a college program.

She was, and is still, involved with the WT volleyball team.

She has a job. I'm sorry, 2 jobs.

She has her own section of the house, which she doesn't want to leave!

She has all of the friends a person could ever want, who would be there for her at the drop of a hat.

Hali has one of the richest lives a person could ever imagine having, but to be honest, it has taken a lot of work to get her to that point.

And just when you think your life is becoming normalized, reality sets in, and you hit a minor speedbump. We can't escape these reminders, but it's also during these times that we find reasons to celebrate, and in our family, we celebrate big!

All we can do is keep marching along in our purpose, and finding the joy in living our story!

Justin Thompson

Chapter 7: The Talk

We all know what "The Talk" is, but you know you have a Hali, when:

"The Talk" is about how your family is going to be different from most, and it's not about that other thing. It also means that "The Talk" should really be called "The Multiple Talks" because it's an ongoing conversation that occurs every time we go through the seasons of life and those differences are realized.

The first time I ever became aware of this difference was when Hali began having severe seizures. Our rooms were close together and she had an old wooden frame that made a noise every time she moved. After that first time, I had a hard time going to sleep at night. I would lay in bed waiting to hear the bed start shaking so I could run to tell my parents.

For the most part, I was probably already awake, because I was in training to be a great college student who operates on little sleep. I never really liked to go to sleep in the first place because I was afraid that I might miss something, which is true even to this day.

Even since having our daughter I will stay awake after we put her to bed just so I get the sense that I got every minute out of that day that I could. And, who are we kidding, that episode of The Office isn't going to watch itself for the 100th time.

In the early days, my parents would have to take her to the emergency room, because we didn't know what was happening. Then after she was diagnosed, it still happened because she was out-growing her medication levels frequently, which is something you don't really think about until you have to. I never really freaked out about anything; it just seemed like that's what our family did.

Hali is only 18 months younger than me, so I have never known a life without her. Plus, Mom and Dad would have to call our friend, Kyle, over to watch me, but even that wasn't terrible because he'd let me stay up and it was like a mid-week sleepover with a friend! We created a lot of stories during those times.

Starting at that point, Kyle would become one of the most influential people in my life. He is the perfect mentor because I can't fool him. He has literally watched me grow up and there isn't anything I wouldn't trust him with. It is important to have those people in your life!

The issues, though, would come the next day. I wouldn't have any idea what time my parents would make it back home, but somehow I was always awake and ready for school the next day. That was probably the time I realized how different my life was compared to my friends. If the other kids were tired at school, it wasn't because of their sister.

Our journey has always looked a little different than most. I can remember a time in high school when I was upset about something that happened because we have Hali. I can't remember what caused it to come about, there were several things that happened that may have led to the conversation. My mom came into my room and apologized because our family wasn't normal. My heart broke. I remember thinking, "What is 'normal'?"

My normal looked a lot like this…

Once I received my driver's license, I became Hali's driver. We went to the same school so it really wasn't a big deal, except when it came to the choice of music. I self-admittedly like to listen to my music on full blast. I don't want to even have an idea of what is going on around me if I'm listening to music. I also tend to listen to most forms of rock, ranging from the classics all the way up until the rock of my youth. (I have, for the most part, cut off listening to anything that came after I graduated college.)

This would, of course, start a heated debate on how loud my music was and it would continue until we got to school. The conversation would then switch from music to an argument about where I parked.

To be fair, I did park quite a ways from the front doors, but I had a good reason. Those spots were never fought over, I ended every day in the field house so it made sense for me to be parked closer to the field house, and I am terrible at parking. Hali didn't agree with this thought process, especially when it started getting cold. Then, one day, it all changed for her.

I received my very own handicap-parking placard. We had one in each car because Hali's stamina was starting to decrease and at the time we didn't know why. We just knew that if we went somewhere that required a lot of walking, our vehicle needed to be close to the exit. Since I drove Hali several places I was honored with one of my own.

Not long after I received Hali's placard, we were driving to school and Hali had a brilliant idea! Yes, this was Hali's idea!! She asked me if we could park up close to the doors and since we had the new "priority parking" sticker, we could get even closer. I gave in to the pressure and we pulled right in. I popped the placard on the rear review mirror and in we walked.

Our newfound joy didn't last long. One of the few problems with going to a smaller school was the fact that the principals knew who drove which cars. I am sitting in one of my morning classes when I get summoned to our assistant principal's office.

I walk proudly down the hall behind the student office helper. As soon as I walk in, our assistant principal smiles at me and asks me to take a seat. He says, "Justin, I know that you bring Hali to school, and that is why you have the handicap sticker. Unfortunately, I also know your parents, and I know that they would have an issue with using it at school. What do you think they would say if I called them and told them about this?"

Of course I knew exactly what they would say.

"So since we both know how that would go, I am just going to ask you to move your truck, and I better not see it in the handicap spaces again."

"Yes sir. I'll get it moved. You know it wasn't my idea!"

He laughed dismissively as I walked out of the office, dejected, but as I got in the truck, I held my head high in pride that, if even for just a moment, we had beaten the system! I will forever take that as a win, no matter how short lived it was, because it's not often that we get to take a victory with Hali's situation. We take several losses, but it makes the victories so much sweeter!

I walked around the halls a legend that day. Everyone knew that it was me who parked in that spot right beside the door. I felt great about the whole thing...

Then I had to go home. I didn't exactly receive a legend's welcome. Apparently, the mastermind of the whole plot had told on me. Needless to say, my placard privileges were taken away and, almost 15 years later, I still don't have them back.

Not many people have a story like that, and even fewer would consider that to be normal. In my life, that kind of thing happened frequently. Hali and I are a great tag team, and while it rarely works out in our favor, we have a great time during the process and we always end up with a great story!

Over the years, I have come to realize that normal is a relative term, and everyone has their own version of normal. There is nothing wrong with that, its just the way it is, and if our family had been "normal" we wouldn't be where we are today. Our path was changed dramatically when Hali was given to us.

Yes, Hali has a disability. Yes, there are things that Hali can't do because of it. But, not for one second, can we ever become frozen in that belief. When we are frozen in that reality, we miss an amazing life that is out there to be lived. My reality is that "The Talk" was about having a sister with special needs, and what that would mean for our family. But, you know what?

If it wasn't my reality, I wouldn't be writing this book, and I definitely wouldn't be in a line of work that allows me to help people reach their maximum potential.

We all have those moments in our lives that define our journey. You can try to run away from it, I mean I tried, but if you do, you may miss out on an extraordinary opportunity to change someone's life!

Justin Thompson

Chapter 8: Wedding Gift

What was the strangest gift you have ever received?

The moment you are asked that question, you immediately begin to think through all of the birthday and Christmas gifts that you have accumulated over the years. I am sure that you have a list that could compete with anyone.

The movie, The Christmas Story, comes to my mind when I think of strange gifts. One of the best moments is when Ralphie walks down the stairs in his new gift from his aunt. A pink bunny costume. He looks miserable as he strategically stays away from all windows so he won't be seen by the public, and he bolts back up the stairs when he is finally given the go ahead to change out of the costume.

Now that's bad, and I am sure that you can relate.

But, did you ever receive a gift that came with a plus one?

Plus one?

Wait… what?

Monica and I received a wedding gift that came with a plus one. It is a deluxe air mattress with a built-in air pump, and the gift also included a complete bed set. Who was it from you ask? At this point, you should know exactly from whom it came. Hali Thompson. The only way it would have been even better is if she had shown up on our doorstep with bed and sheets in tow with my parents driving away. Our gift was the mattress, and Hali was its plus one.

I know what you are thinking, yes, it is a weird wedding present. It is also weird for someone to give a gift that only they will use when they come to your house. However, it's not weird for the Thompsons. In fact, when we decided on a house the first question from Hali was where her room was going to be. No congratulations, I'm happy for you guys, none of that. Which one is my room!?

That is just part of the territory for us. My parents travel quite a bit and when they don't take Hali, we are the first on a list of MANY to keep her. Now, you need to know that when Hali comes to stay the night with you, its not just her strolling up with a weekender.

No no, she walks through the door with a backpack full of gadgets that Best Buy would be jealous of, a four-inch binder of DVDs so full that she has them stuck in the sides of the binder and the zipper won't shut, and last, but not least, a list of everywhere she needs to be.

That's just the way it is. Hali can do a lot of things on her own, but stay overnight by herself is not one of those things. Although I try to normalize most of our life, this is one area that I can't. It is not typical to have your 28-year old sister live with your parents, and need a place to stay when they go out of town.

It would be fairly easy to run away from this aspect. I mean, it's not like I don't have my own life and family to care for; then for those nights we are adding an extra person. I don't really see it that way, though. For me, one of my brotherly duties is to watch my sister when my parents are out of town, and I don't really think twice about it. Does it change things up a little? Yes. Does it also give us a free babysitter for the night? Absolutely it does! But, I also think that since it's something that has been a part of my life for so long that it's as normal as can be for my life.

Let's be honest, I didn't exactly have a choice to be Hali's brother. I wasn't asked what I would want in a sister for development purposes, and, even if I had, how would I have answered at 18 months old?

It goes back to that comfort level that we talked about. In Hali's life, there are very few things that make me uncomfortable, but that is only because it has been a major part of my entire life.

I guess you can say Monica is the craziest one of us all because she married into it!! I am blessed to have her by my side as we navigate this journey of being Hali Thompson's brother and sister!

It is never easy, but it is usually fun. We can't allow our limitations to keep us from living this life we have been given. We, also, can't allow ourselves to become so exclusive that we don't have room for a plus-one.

I am often guilty of becoming so focused on me that I don't feel like I have room for one more. I live within my exclusive bubble of comfort and contentment while there are people out there who need help. My wife is the exact opposite. For her there is always room for a plus-one. Another gift of hers that has made her the perfect sister-in-law for Hali, she is always thinking of ways to reach out to more people, and bringing them along for the ride.

It may not be typical for you to have your sibling need to come stay at your house, and drive them around to all of the places they need to be, but this is the life we have been given. There isn't anything I can do to change that aspect of it, but I can find the joy in it and use that inclusiveness as a gift for other people. And, in our case, it means that we always have an extra place to sleep.

So remember, if you find yourself needing a place to rest, just hit me up. We have a state-of-the-art air mattress with a built-in air pump and multi-colored paisley sheets!

Chapter 9: Win-Win if Hali Loses

For those who don't know, I am one of the more competitive people you will ever meet. I don't even want to joke around about it, because I don't want you to get the impression that I am even remotely ok with the thought losing. Does this mean I have never taken a loss? No, I have taken plenty in my short time on earth. But, it doesn't mean that I like and want to repeat the process.

To highlight just how far it goes, here is a non-Hali story. My wife wanted us to become healthier. In order to do this, she signed us up for a 6-week challenge with a local fitness group. In order to meet the challenge, we had to lose 20 pounds or 5% body fat while working out and following their meal plan. To be honest, I had sworn off of physical exercise and my diet consisted of whatever I wanted it to.

I was very fearful of the challenge, and then she dropped a little nugget of encouragement that she wasn't even aware of. She said that she didn't think I would be able to meet the weight challenge, but she wanted us to do this to build healthier habits in our life.

Game over.

And, that's all you need to know.

Now, because I thrive in this environment, I had to develop coping strategies for when I lost, especially playing card games because, you're only as good as the cards you are dealt.

Our family plays a lot of games and after years of playing against Hali. I have figured out that I cannot lose when playing with Hali because...

It's not about whether, or not, you lose the UNO game, but instead it's about making sure Hali doesn't win the UNO game. So if Hali loses I still win, setting up the ultimate in win-win situations.

This chapter is a special shout-out to my dad, and I can hear you asking why I am bringing him into this. Well, Dad and I are a team. My dad and I are two peas-in-a-pod. I don't believe that parents should be best friends with their children, until the children become adults, but at this point in my life, I can honestly say, that he has become one of my best friends.

We share a lot of things in common. We watch the same sports and have a continuing dialogue during sporting events. We have often worked in similar fields. And most important, he and my mom survived the time in my life when I absolutely knew everything about everything.

It is only fitting that we team up during the family UNO game.

Our number one goal is to make sure that she doesn't win, because remember, it's a win-win when Hali loses. If we happen to win in this pursuit ... that's not a bad thing, either. But, in a bit of honesty, I must also let you know that the line between fair play and cheating becomes blurry, if not washed out.

Before you begin to side with Hali you need to know a couple of things.

Hali is a Thompson, which means she's just as competitive as the rest of us. She even takes it to the extreme! Every time a holiday approaches I give my sister a text informing her that I will be off on that Friday, because you know I am not competitive at all, and her response to me is always, "Oh yeah, well I get every Friday, off plus the same holiday you get off!"

DO YOU SEE WHAT WE'RE DEALING WITH HERE?

Also, someone needs to knock her off her pedestal. I mean everywhere we go its Queen Hali here, and we will do whatever for Miss H-Baby there. I can sum it up for you in this short story.

Hali was the manager for the Canyon volleyball team during high school and in high school, parents typically call the lines during the game. Often, my dad would volunteer so that the other parents could watch their kids play, and it's not like he doesn't know the sport. His twin aunts were the all-time winningest active coaches in Texas at one point. We know the game.

So my dad steps in to his new role and starts calling the lines. Everything was going great until a few close calls went against Hali's belief. Yes, I say belief, because the right call is all about perspective. If it's called for you then it's a great call, but if it goes against, then it's a bad call. After several points went against Canyon, the coach calls a timeout.

Instead of Hali being the encouraging team manager and joining her team, she storms toward Dad and yells, "Do you know what this means?!?" signalling the sign for a ball that landed in.

Dad responds, "Yes, Hali I do."

To which Queen Hali says, "REALLY, BECAUSE I DON'T THINK YOU DO!!"

It was a brief exchange because Hali started to feel the all-knowing glare that Mom was giving her, and she quickly re-joined her team in the huddle.

In fact, I have often thought about starting a membership organization entitled, The Hali Thompson Humility Squad. There would be membership dues, but all proceeds would go to local non-profits serving individuals with special needs. To officially become a member you must pass through an extensive training to build mental fortitude against the charms of one Hali Thompson. If you're interested, hit me up.

You see, UNO is one of our only chances, as the only men in our immediate family, to exact redemption.

Should you feel sorry for her...

NO!!

It's UNO which means that Hali is able to lay her cards face up on the table and still win because she is the queen at lucking out. I'm serious. She shows her cards to her opponents and still comes away victorious. If that isn't frustrating, then I don't know what is.

In our families we seem to always be striving for some sense of normalcy. We look at what other families are doing, and we think that we need to be doing that as well. The truth is, how we create our sense of normalcy will look different from yours. Games are a big part of our normalcy and UNO is the main player. It is during those games we get a chance to laugh, have fun and, most important, be together. Even through some of the hardest times, we have played several games in the hospital. And, while our relationship may look a little different than some, our sibling rivalry is just as strong as anyone's.

Being Hali's brother brings me into a class of my own, it requires more as a sibling than most. It means that I am way too comfortable with hospitals, seizures, and medications.

But, even in those moments it also means that I can, also, still be her brother, and if I'm able to get one over on her I can always bust out our pack of UNO. Life is serious enough; we don't have to add to it.

Justin Thompson

Chapter 10: The Pick Up List

At this point, we have covered the fact that Hali is a busy person. We know that she has two jobs, helps with volleyball at West Texas A&M University, and watches kids in the children's wing at our church. And, by now, you have probably figured out that she can't drive.

There have been two instances when we thought we would let her venture out and have control of a wheel. The first time happened when we were in elementary school. We were in the big metropolis of Clarendon, Texas helping our great-grandparents move from their farm into town. During one break, our papa took us over to the local go-kart track. At the time, we were both old enough to drive on our own, and the track didn't have any two-seaters for someone to drive Hali.

A little side-note: my parents learned what Hali could and couldn't do through trial and error. It is something that I now respect greatly because it takes great faith as a parent to ask the question, "How do we know for sure if she hasn't tried it?"

So, Hali hops in the driver's seat. Luckily for us, she was really cautious, and she was doing great, until our turn ended. At that point, she had to pull in the bays right behind the kart in front of her, but she had to make a split-second decision, right or left side? Well, Hali didn't choose. She slams into the median and I am too close behind her to stop so I slam into the back of her kart.

Everything seems to be ok, until she gets out of the seat, and she is bleeding from the back of her head. Unfortunately, there was a part of the headrest that hadn't been covered and it split her head. My parents put her in the car and headed to the closest medical facility, which wasn't Clarendon at the time. Hali ultimately received stitches for her efforts, and I had to get back to work.

The second time, also, came while we were in Clarendon helping our papa build fence on his farm. See the theme here?

We are out in the field walking up and down the fence line driving posts and placing wires, and in a moment of brilliance, I got the idea that we could speed up the process if Hali used the 4-wheeler to carry things back and forth to me. I walked her through everything she needed to know and she was ready. I put it in gear and stepped back. Hali slams on the throttle, hits one of the rows in the field and the 4-wheeler takes a sharp right turn... without Hali. I run to the scene and Hali bounces right up and lets me know she's alright.

After I knew she wasn't phased, I looked at the section of fence I had just built. I guess I hadn't done it correctly, because the 4-wheeler undid everything I had just finished. Moral of the story? If you're going to teach Hali how to drive anything with a motor, make sure it's in the middle of an open field and not next to the fence you were building.

Needless to reiterate, Hali doesn't drive.

One of Hali's jobs is at a Montessori day-care, and each child has a strict list of people who are allowed to pick them up. And, because the kids have a list then she needs to have one as well, and the people who pick her up need to be on it. But it doesn't end there.

Every week Monica and I get asked if we need to be on her list. Trust me, we've been added. Several times in fact, but that is only the tip of the iceberg. After we determine that she can add us on the list, we then move down the family tree. We cover any possible scenario in which there is no one left to pick her up, except Monica's 10th cousin by marge (spelled marriage in general English). I say it in those terms because Hali loves family history and her favorite aspect is "by marge," as it would show up on your phone.

Why do we need to be on her list? Because just about every Wednesday we pick her up and take her to eat before church. Outside of Wednesdays, we pick her up from time to time when my parents aren't able to do it.

I have to say, just about, because apparently we don't pick her up often enough (we pick her up 19 out of 20 Wednesdays) for her to feel confident in us. So, we have a day long conversation every Wednesday about if we are picking her up.

Every now and then we decide to return the favor and we start sending her messages asking if we are getting her that night. This effort results in an afternoon of texting and the eventual message from Hali that she is shutting off her phone for a bit.

Now you may be wondering why this is so important to Hali. Well for starters, her job is to make sure that only the people on the list are allowed to pick up their kids. Side note: you don't want to try your luck on that one; if you don't believe me, there are a couple of people who are probably still very upset that she wouldn't let them, and I'm sure they would love to tell you about it!

More importantly, in all honesty, Hali doesn't have much control over the things that typical adults have control over. The one thing that Hali knows she has control over is her schedule.

She knows where she needs to be, what time, how long she needs to be there, and who is getting her there. Other than her niece, her schedule may be the most important thing to her.

While I understand it, from both life/work experience and different classes I have taken over the years, it still creates a little friction.

You could say this is one of the things where Hali and I clash. Every week after several texts messages I often want to write back, Hali, we do this every week. The weeks that I don't pick you up, we tell you ahead of time and we make sure Mom or Dad will pick you up. Or, yes, Hali add Monica to the list and don't ask again!!!!!!!

Now the beauty of text messaging is that it has a little built in filter that slows me down enough to not press send. I do think about it, though.

I know she can't help it, and I also know that she knows who is going to be where and what they are doing. But, just because I can understand it and accept that she can't really help it, doesn't mean it can't frustrate me.

Sometimes she frustrates me! Let me say it again, sometimes my sister, Hali, frustrates me!

And being the great brother I am, I return the frustration with a retaliation like the one above.

At the end of the day, I think this is another one of the things that make us a typical brother and sister. Sometimes we feel a pressure to not act this way because of our special situation, but even in that, our special situation doesn't exempt us from being brother and sister. It doesn't keep us from getting into it in the car on a family trip and having to walk down the road holding hands as our punishment. (I'll unpack that one for y'all later.)

The pressure to believe this way is real and sometimes overwhelming. Hali may be the reason that I, personally, feel this way, but we all have circumstance where we begin to feel guilty in a situation where we don't think we should. The guilt comes from a perception that during these times, our natural feelings are to be set aside until a more appropriate time comes along.

Take it from a non-expert, it's ok to have these feelings, and there's an appropriate time. It's ok to be frustrated, from time to time, with how things are going, but it's as important to work through that, because if you find yourself in that position all the time, it can lead to a path you might not want to go down.

And when it's appropriate, respond to that frustration with a little humor!

Chapter 11: Fan Section

I would like to let you in on a little secret that not many people know, and it will come as a shock because I am one of the more introverted people you will meet.

I would love nothing more than to have one opportunity to be in front of a crowd of thousands of people cheering me on.

My mind usually goes to golf because I can picture, in my mind, standing on the final green with a chance to win the tournament. There I am, standing with thousands of my newest close friends, with a chance to hear them cheer for me!

This will never happen, and I don't lose sleep over it. I just think it would an awesome experience, and I have had a similar experience my entire life.

One of the true blessings of having a Hali is that she brought me into a community that has been my fan section for many years.

In high school, every Friday night home game I had the honor of running through the tunnel in front of my own personal fan club! I would love to tell you that it was because I am special, but I highly doubt that is the reason.

Because of Hali I had grown up being very involved with Special Olympics, and more importantly, I had the opportunity to grow up with our guys. Hali introduced me into a world where I became, for the most part, a surrogate brother to Hali's friends, and when I reached high school sports, they couldn't wait to cheer me on.

It was an incredible and humbling experience that I not only had the opportunity to play football, but I had the opportunity to do it for a group of people who never got that same chance.

Another layer of being Hali's Brother is that I am not just Hali's Brother. I am also Katie's Brother, Jacob's Brother, Tommy's Brother, Omar's Brother, Dominique's Brother, Paul's Brother, Kylie's Brother, Joe's brother, Tanner's brother and the list goes on. I am as connected to this community as I am to Hali.

Which means I get to celebrate a lot! But, it also means that I go through some heartaches as well.

I've grown up knowing that I not only represent myself and my family, but an entire community as well. With that comes the reality that I don't get to pick and choose when I want to be a part of our community.

I am in it through the pain of losing one of ours, just as I am in it when one of ours gets that new job that they have been asking us to pray about for weeks.

It always hurts when we have to say goodbye. For Hali and me, our first time was when Hali was in kindergarten and I was in the second grade. Eric was his name. He was actually in my grade so we had music and P.E. together, but he was also in Hali's special education class. He loved music class and when we would start, he got the biggest smile on his face!

It was a struggle to understand losing Eric at such a young age. As I have matured it has become even more of a struggle. I find myself constantly asking the question, why?

The hard truth is that I will probably never know exactly why. I can rationalize it. I can hear from other people that this is part of their story, but that doesn't really help at times.

No matter how I am feeling, I truly believe that when The Story is revealed, we will understand it. We will understand it when we see the change brought about through Eric's life, through Kylie's life, through Hali's life, and through her brother's life.

We all represent a community. We all belong to a group bigger than any individual. Through that community we bring in our story to make it only that much better.

I have to believe this. Hali's life brings about too many hard times to not.

So I will ask you the same question that has been asked of me on several occasions. What are the things that you are contributing to your community? If you don't know yet, that's not a problem, but I'd ask you, what are the things in your life that are unique to you?

When you discover that uniqueness, it opens the door for your contribution. And you, being at the table, is the only way it will ultimately work.

There are plenty of people similar to me in this world. They have a sister with special needs, have a similar skillset as me, and they grew up with similar experiences. But, what they don't have is my story. My story is unique to only me, because nobody else is Hali's Brother as I am Hali's Brother.

The best part about this is that it's the same thing for Hali, for Jacob, for Tommy, for their families, and it's the same thing for you!

There is an older theory in Social Work that can be used when working with communities, and larger groups of people, which states that an organism can't operate at its maximum potential until all of the pieces are both represented and contributing. When the Hali's of the world are left out of the picture, our larger community suffers.

If you are not representing and contributing, we suffer. You can't bake something and expect it turn out perfect if you leave out an ingredient, yet we seem to be ok with doing that same thing in our local communities.

It's scary, and it takes a lot strength to step out there, but just know that when you do, there's a huge cheering section just waiting for you right outside the tunnel!!

We all need a fan-section, but it is something that we have to cultivate. Who is in your fan section? And are they still cheering for you even when you're the most average person on the field?

Justin Thompson

Chapter 12: Social Butterfly… Until She's Not

I just need you to know that she started it!

Sound familiar? It was a common phrase which was used in the Thompson household. In fact, it happened enough to where typical punishments were no longer effective. I joke with people when they ask if we have any other siblings by saying, Hali and I were enough.

My parents had to be very creative in their punishments for us as we were growing up. Unfortunately, for us, both of my parents were going to college and working on degrees in Counseling and Psychology while we were growing up. If you aren't familiar with that situation, it means that they were studying us in the context of what they were studying in school. We got everything! Later, on as a teenager, I would have to tell my dad that I needed my dad and not the counselor. It worked well.

My favorite creative punishment was the classic behavior modification technique. In our house, we used quarters. Each week we would start out with a certain amount of money, and every time we would get in trouble, we had to hand over a quarter.

I did well, for the most part, but my biggest expense was talking back to my parents. I was very confident in my stance and wasn't afraid to voice my opinion. When I would start to argue, my parents would stop me and tell me to go get my quarters. The first time offense was just one quarter, but that meant I would not have an opportunity to continue my argument. Being the smart person that I am, I figured that if it was going to cost me then I was going to make it worth it. Therefore, I would grab two quarters. I would give them both to my mom and let her know that I was paying it upfront because I was going to say whatever I wanted.

For some reason, I never had much money left at the end of the week.

To get a clearer picture, you need to know what generally led to our disagreements. In one corner you had me, and I have never backed down from an argument. I was going to get the last word, and I was going to win. It's one of my many fine qualities.

And Hali? Well, Hali wasn't going to lose either, as you already know. So something would happen to start the fight, the bell would ring, and there we stood in the middle of the ring ready to throw down. I don't know how many of you have watched a boxing match, but picture this. The bell rings to start the round.

The fighters come to the middle, and for the next three minutes, they trade hits (in our case, words.) Then the bell would ring to end the round. At some point during the match, the fighters will have to be separated because they are fighting after the bell. Each boxer's team rushes to the ring to pull his guy back to the corner. But, you can't let the other guy get the last word, so you see them, as they're being held back, turn around and keep shouting at their opponent.

That's us. Hali going to her room still arguing her case, and me going to mine doing the same thing.

Eventually, my parents grew very tired of this, and decided to start making us take a walk together holding hands. Usually, there was a certain distance that we had to cover to be done, and being the great brother I am, I would drag Hali behind me to finish as fast as I could.

This cruel punishment wasn't limited to arguments at home. Hali and I have walked together on many road trips. Once we had to walk down a highway between Tulsa, Oklahoma and Arkansas. I mean, I guess it was safe. Mom and Dad followed right behind us with the flashers blinking.

For me, this was humiliating, because I hated to be the center of attention, and this most definitely drew attention! I don't mind the attention so much now, but back then it was miserable!

On this particular occasion, we made the mistake of starting an argument in Wal-Mart. We got into it, and my parents went right to their quiver of punishment arrows and made us walk around Wal-Mart holding hands. This time was different. There wasn't a set amount of time or distance, instead, we had to do this until Hali ran into someone she knew…

I was thinking this was a win for us because everyone knew Hali in Canyon, TX. And, I knew that even if Hali didn't recognize the person she would play it off like she did, and afterwards, she would tell Mom and Dad how she knew them. We were golden!!

What we didn't know is that apparently there was a memo sent out to avoid the Canyon Wal-Mart on this night because we didn't see anyone! I mean you couldn't even coordinate such a movement today with social media. How is it that we didn't see one person that we knew? It's not like there were other options besides Wal-Mart. We even made the mistake of having this argument at the beginning of the shopping experience! What were we thinking?

I couldn't believe this was happening to me! I mean, here we are, Hali Thompson who prides herself on how many friends she has, and she doesn't know a single person!!

Are you kidding me? How does this happen?

Oh, and sure, the next time we went she knew everyone! How convenient.

You know what's funny about this, it didn't stop us. We had more arguments the next day, and the next, and we still do. Poor Monica doesn't know what to do when we get into it.

In a moment of self-disclosure, these days I am usually the one who instigates, because well... I just like pushing her buttons sometimes.

The interesting thing about Hali that she likes being in the middle of everything, but she doesn't like being the center of attention. Once she feels the attention, she backs away. We share in that together. I have no problem being in the shadows, but I also don't mind the attention from time to time.

You would think that as much as Hali likes being in the middle of everything that she would love being the center of attention, which would be a great thing for speaking in front of people. We have had the great opportunity to speak to folks, as siblings, on different occasions. Early on, we thought this would be right up her alley, but we quickly discovered that it causes her to get anxious.

As for me, I am very introverted, which means being around people drains my energy instead of refilling it, as it would for extroverts. I had to figure this out, just like we had to figure it out with Hali.

Being created a certain way doesn't mean that you are only limited to doing one set of things; what it means is that you have to know yourself and how those things will impact you.

Hali and I love speaking to people, and will do it as long as we're invited. Knowing ourselves allows us to prepare properly. When we don't take time to know ourselves, or we forget, we get burned out and we lose hope, and when you have a Hali those two things are not optional.

Chapter 13: The Apology is More Painful

I am sure that we have all had moments when we were faced with a decision, and our decision is based on how much effort will be required. We ask ourselves, is it worth it? Like, I really want that third apple fritter, but is it worth it to be miserable for the next several hours? In my case, yes.

One of the more common worth it decisions, for me, is this. You know you have a Hali when the process of the apology far exceeds the discomfort caused by her making a mistake.

Hali doesn't forget when she messes up, and when I say she doesn't forget, I mean she doesn't forget. One time she sent me a text apologizing for something that happened so long ago that I had to ask her what she was talking about!

There are only two times when my text messaging plan even gets close to its limit:

1. When my parents are out of town and Hali is in our care.

2. When Hali feels like she has done something wrong.

This time both were about to happen at the same time.

Tensions were already mounting as we had two storms approaching. Ella had been sick off and on for about a month, which meant Justin and Monica hadn't slept very much, and Hali had already spent a week with us and was about to spend another couple of nights. Not really a big deal at all; it just helps my story to present it that way. Plus it is my book.

We came home from Pizza Night at the church and were all done for the night. We put Ella to bed and she went to sleep without any fight. Then it's Hali's turn.

Hali decided to exercise her right to stay up until 10:15 because that's her bedtime and, even though she was falling asleep in her chair, she wasn't going to bed before her bedtime. Hali's room shares a wall with Ella's room. I think you know where I'm going.

Hali opens the door, which sticks, so it's loud.

She closes it.

She comes back out to go to the restroom.

She goes back into the room.

She comes back out to tell us good night, and not in a whisper.

She goes back in and knocks over some shelves.

She comes out to tell me that she's ok.

Then wants to have a conversation about it.

She finally goes back in for the last time.

We hold our breath for a moment, then we hear it.

Ella has awaken!

I spend the next hour rocking her back to sleep.

Needless to say I was livid, and was tempted to let Ella keep crying because I knew that Hali could hear her, but that would just punish us.

The next morning I'm in the kitchen weighing my options of confronting Hali. I already knew that I was going to be receiving several messages from her throughout the day.

I also knew if we had this conversation on the way to work that she would feel so bad that she'd start crying. Having been there before, I wanted to avoid that situation as much as possible. Hali is not a gentle crier.

Ok, decision made. Telling Hali that she woke up Ella last night was not going to be worth the hours of apology texts and Niagra Falls of tears.

We did address it, however, by having some house rules in place the next time she stayed overnight.

So why does Hali feel the need to apologize so much? There are a couple reasons.

She has to have closure. Much like the rest of us, she doesn't want to leave anything open-ended. If there is going to be a start, then there will be an ending. If you ever watch a movie with her, it is an experience you will never forget. She watches the first few scenes that set everything up.

Then she moves on to her favorite scenes, sometimes playing them back repeatedly. To finish, she fast-forwards all the way to the end and watches the, always, happy ending. I'm quite certain that there is not a more efficient way of watching a movie. You get the overall scope, watch your favorite scenes, then the ending. There's no need to waste your time on all of the "fillers." She needs closure, and she needs it sooner rather than later.

But, the main reason why is because she has a huge heart! She hates the thought of having wronged someone and them being mad at her. If she has done something that would warrant an apology, she knows that she has messed up, and there is a chance that you may be mad or angry with her.

She can't have that so she tries to clear it up as soon as possible, and if you choose not to respond, she will continue to apologize until you acknowledge her. Even after that, it's a 50/50 shot that the apologies will stop.

We have talked quite a bit about normalcy already, and what better way to experience it than muttering your thoughts about how ticked you are at your sister while you're rocking your daughter back to sleep??

I would love nothing more than to always get along with my sister, and to never have a feeling of frustration with her, but that's just not going to happen. And it would only make things harder on both of us if I pretended like it should always be a fairytale because she has special needs.

I don't know about you, but when I look back on my life I see a lot of time wasted on things that didn't really matter. Sure, we all have moments when we do something for the heck of it, and that's not what I am talking about. I'm talking about those things that consistently take energy away from the things for which you were created.

For the longest time we were told that in order to become stronger we needed to spend more time working on our weaknesses.

It wasn't until I was in college that I heard for the first time that we should consider spending more time perfecting our strengths. This was a great revelation for me. It's possible to focus so much time and energy on what we don't do well, that our strengths become neglected.

Does this mean that we shouldn't work on our weaknesses at all? No, there will always be things that we have to do that aren't in our wheelhouse; that's just part of life.

What are the things that are stealing energy away from your strengths? And in the end, is it worth it?

Justin Thompson

Chapter 14: Tag, You're It

Recess was the greatest part of my day growing up. Usually one of my friends would bring a football, but on the rare occasion when we would forget, we would have to resort to the classic game of tag. Unfortunately, tag didn't necessarily highlight my athleticism in elementary school. I was slow, but I wasn't shifty, either. I spent a lot of time being "it," and eventually I would just have to give up so my friends would have to pick someone else.

However, when you have a Hali, "tag, you're it" involves way more than running after someone. It actually involves a strategic use of timing and availability, very similar to figuring out where she sits during a funeral.

We've talked about the fact that Hali takes things very hard, and knowing that about her means that we have to be very precise about how to break hard news to her. Unfortunately, we have had a lot of practice in this area.

In 2011, we lost our papa unexpectedly. My mom had received the call from the Donley County Sheriff's office because everyone else was out of town, so then she had the duty of reaching out to everyone including, our grandmother, Nanny, who was in Arizona helping with a church camp.

Hali was with our dad in Denver coming back from a conference where they had been speakers. They got the call in the middle of the airport, which meant that Dad had been tagged and he was it for the next several hours. He did his best to get Hali to a quieter spot so she could let all of her emotions out semi-privately.

Being "it" in a Hali situation requires a fairly unique set of skills. You are thrust into a situation where you are part crisis intervention, which helps de-escalate the immediate issue, and part consoler, which provides comfort during the very loud cry of my sister.

As I have said before, I don't understand it at all, but it seems like we have to go through this event too often. The hardest part for me isn't the impact on myself, but the toll it takes on Hali.

Monica and I were getting ready to go on vacation and Ella was set to stay with my parents. It was a regular Tuesday, which meant that my mom was going to pick up Ella from mother's day out. We went to work as we would any other day, I sat down for lunch with coworkers before a meeting, and my phone begins to ring. I see that it's my mom and I have a few minutes before the meeting starts so I walk out to the hallway to answer it.

I don't know if my mom knows this, but I can always tell when it's not going to be a pleasant conversation. She asks in a very specific tone, "Hey, do you have a minute?"

At that moment, I knew that my day was about to look very different from what I originally thought. Some of my parents' best friends had called and updated them on the progress on their grandson, Noah, who had been born prematurely. Since the day he was born, you knew he was a fighter because of everything he was overcoming with each minute. Then overnight, he developed an infection and the prognosis wasn't very good.

My parents needed to make the emergency drive down to Lubbock to be with their friends, and weren't going to be able to pick up Ella or Hali. Yes, this was one of the days that she works, but you already knew that because I know you remember her schedule. It wasn't any problem at all for me to do both of those things so I quickly volunteered as soon as she asked. We hung up and I went back to my meeting.

Ten minutes after the meeting started, I get another phone call. This time I really can't answer it, so I let it go to voicemail. About 5 minutes after I get the voicemail alert I get a text from my dad that there wasn't a need to call them back because the voicemail said it all.

I answered with my classic response of "Right On" and finished the meeting. As soon as the meeting finished, I rushed out to listen to my message, and sure enough it was all I needed to know. They had not told Hali because she was at work, and Mom couldn't be there to comfort her, and they weren't going to let her know that I was going to be the one who picked her up.

In other words, "Tag, you're it."

It was going to be left up to me to give her the bad news. It was hard for me to be frustrated about it because I knew that it was exactly what we had to do. We all know that when Hali receives bad news, you can only try to console her. She lets out this big loud cry and there's no bringing it back until she is finished. We didn't want her to have to go through it at work without any of us there.

As soon as I finished the message I called them back anyway and told them, "You know you have a Hali when you get a detailed voicemail laying out the plan for telling her."

It's usually my mom who has to bear the brunt of the emotional breakdown, so I wasn't upset at all when it became my turn. I also had a sense of relief about the situation because I knew I would have the secret weapon with me when I picked her up… Ella!

It breaks my heart watching her go through that, because I know how much she cares about others.

I get myself in trouble, though, when I need to tag someone else, but don't. So often in running our race, we start thinking that we have to do everything on our own, which is simply just not true.

Being Hali's only sibling means that at times I feel like I have to be able to do everything for my sister, and I eventually lead myself to exhaustion. I don't know if it's the spirit of individualism, or what, but in my early adult years I have had to re-wire my thinking about community.

Instead of tagging someone else, I continue to go at a pace that I can't keep, because growing up with a sister like Hali always made me feel like I needed to fill in where my parents couldn't. I still struggle with this because I feel like this is my situation, and I shouldn't cast my burdens onto someone else. Therefore, it's like I'm trying to run a marathon at a sprinter's speed and pace. There is one major problem with that; running at a sprinters pace means I won't finish the race.

More than anything, Hali needs me to be there for her in the future, and if I don't take care of myself now, I can't guarantee that I will. As a brother, that is a terrifying thought. We have to be ok with reaching out for help. The hard truth is that I can't do it all on my own, and neither can you. Tag someone else and give yourself a break!

Justin Thompson

Chapter 15: You See It When You Believe It

Do you remember those times on the playground when one of your friends would come up to you and tell you this big outrageous story about what happened to them? What was your typical response?

If you are anything like me, it was either "Oh yeah, prove it," or it was "I'll believe it when I see it." This wasn't ever a short conversation, either, because immediately your friend would start to make their case about how you just needed to believe them. Before you knew it, recess was over and you had wasted the entire time talking, instead of playing. Bitter.

Do you ever wonder if we have been saying that phrase wrong this entire time?

Hali was riding home with my parents after church on a Sunday, and I can't remember what actually started the conversation, but Hali responded with "I'll see it when I believe it."

Wait a minute... that's not right, or is it? When Mom called me to tell what she had said, we all took a moment and talked about how perfect that statement is, even though it's completely backwards from it's original saying.

I don't know if there is a better metaphor for our lives then a phrase said in the wrong order, carrying more weight than if it was said correctly. We go about our lives thinking that everything needs to happen a certain way, but what happens when that gets disrupted? For the Thompsons, that came with Hali.

When Hali came into the world, my parents had a picture of how they thought their life would look, and, up until this point, there hadn't been anything that would have shown them any different. Has it been easy? Not at all, but it hasn't been a bad journey, either.

Along this journey, we have heard "you can't" and "you won't" a lot. I have heard my parents tell a lot of stories about the early days of Hali's journey, but one story sticks out to me as the turning point in our family's story.

We were fortunate in that Hali was born at a time when inclusion was coming around. Through the hard work and dedication of several people before her, doors were starting to open for Hali that would not have previously been there. However, the old way of thinking about disabilities was still prevalent in a lot of places. So when the diagnostician sat down with my parents, she delivered the news in the way that she perceived they would take it. She provided it as a worst-case scenario, immediately squashing a parent's hope for their child.

My parents had no idea what any of this meant at the time. Why would they? So when the diagnostician informed them of the diagnosis, my parents had to ask what that meant. They were told that because of her diagnosis she would never go to college, never live on her own, never get married, and never have children. Looking at it now, it's a shame that those were the things, which she thought, determined a fulfilling life.

It turns out that those were just the words that my parents needed to hear. Not accepting what someone else deemed to be impossible eventually allowed my parents to start asking, "How can we make this happen?" Now they didn't walk out of the meeting, smiling, with a feeling of how great their experience was. They were devastated, and had no idea what to do next.

It wasn't until they learned about a special education class at Gene Howe Elementary, and met Mrs. Mac, that they began to look at the possibilities for Hali. The picture painted by Mrs. Mac was completely different from that of the diagnostician. There was hope, there was an opportunity for joy, and there was an expectation, not just a dream, of a fulfilling life.

I would say that is the moment my parents began seeing it because they started to believe it, and guess who had a front row ticket to all of this? You guessed it, Hali's Brother.

Now, I have to tell you that these were difficult times. And it wouldn't be the only difficult season in our story, but this is where it all started. Very early on, as the sibling, I had to understand that sometimes decisions had to be made that were best for Hali. Which meant that I also had to move schools. We went to 3 different elementary schools without even moving houses! Each time making a move that was best for Hali.

Then there were the times when I put so much pressure on myself to be perfect so my parents didn't have to take attention away from Hali that I made myself sick. That was middle school… high school… somewhat through college, although the things I did would say otherwise, and … yeah I still struggle with that. After many years of trial and error, I had to ask myself the question, what's my purpose in all of this?

Was my purpose to only be Hali's brother? Or was there more? I struggled with believing my purpose for a long time, and because of that, I felt lost. I felt like I was just wandering aimlessly through life while watching others live out their purpose. It wasn't until I truly began believing that I was created for a specific purpose that I started to see how it could be done.

Growing up with Hali isn't always fun, but it's always interesting! Being Hali's brother has brought me into a life that I could have never imagined. Even though I don't know what life is like without Hali, I do know that this book would not become a reality.

These stories would not be the same. I wouldn't have a perspective in this world as unique as I do, and I probably wouldn't have had the same gifts that I do. We were all given gifts to change the lives of others, but we have to use them! And, we can only use them once we believe in ourselves enough to be confident in our seat at the table.

Our life has been great! Hali has brought so much joy and laughter to our lives, and while we go through our share of rocky times, there is always joy to be found. There are always times when we can turn away from the challenges and become bitter about our situation; honestly, you probably have a right to be bitter at times.

When Hali is lying in a hospital bed for the 25th night in a row, or when we have to cut our time short at Disneyland so she can rest, where do we find joy in that? How about when she has to stay the night with you because she can't live on her own? Then there are the times when I would be the only one who could hear her having a seizure; what about then? How about the time you saw and heard someone walk by her in the hallway at school and call her stupid?

Or the time when she fell down and you watched people laugh at her? There's also the time in the grocery store line when people stared at her like she was contagious.

It's hard. It's really hard.

But, what about the times when we're gathered around a table playing games? Or, when she gets a standing ovation from my high school football team as she's wheeled up front with a shaved head and scars to accept an appreciation award from my coaches? OH! Then there's the time when she got to pin her old volleyball coach during her nurse's pinning ceremony.

When she held her niece for the first time, when she gets hugs from her kids at work, when she walks across the stage at a university graduation to receive her certificate of completion...

How can I forget the time when one of her friends asked for special permission to be able to sit by Hali during high school graduation because she had lost her dad unexpectedly the previous fall, and she wanted to sit by the one person who always brought joy back to her life?

Even in the midst of darkness, we can find joy. Sometimes it's barely there. Maybe it's been covered up by years of frustrations, being told no, or bitterness, but it's there. There is no such thing as absolute darkness because light will always be able to penetrate, no matter how small the light is.

Hali Thompson was created for a specific purpose and she was given to the Thompsons for a specific purpose, but so was Justin. Once I believed it, I saw it.

You see it... When you believe it.

ABOUT THE AUTHOR

Justin is a Strategic Analyst for Cal Farley's Boys Ranch. Though he wanted to do his own thing early on, growing up with Hali led him back to school where he earned his Master's in Social Work from West Texas A&M University. Though his career has taken a path different than he originally thought, he is very active with the Hali Project in serving adults with special needs on their monthly social nights, and as a kitchen assistant during his parents' (Brad and Karen) marriage retreats. The true blessing is serving alongside his wife, Monica, and daughter, Ella. In his downtime, he practices his craft as the Chair of the Hali Thompson Humility Squad.